HAVE YOUR CAKE
AND EAT IT TOO

April Vargo

This book is dedicated to my amazing family. Thank you Jason, Dad, Mom, Bill, and Madeline. You have all been my rocks and the foundation for who I am today. I love you all so much! This one's for you!

PLAYSINGACT LLC   2019

CONTENTS

THE FINAL STRAW

I'm 30 years old standing in the middle of my classroom wondering how I got here. I had been teaching for eight years and this was by far my worst year to date.

I was working in an urban school, which I always thought would be my dream school, but quickly turned nightmare. Many of my students were involved in gangs, initiations were on the rise - many occurring in our building. We had to go through staff trainings on how to defend ourselves if our students chose to attack us, and learn the gang colors and signs.

I had the pleasure of being told my classroom would be used as a space to help kids get out of gangs. This program brought in ex-cons to try and reach these children, in hopes of saving them. I was asked to sit in the room at first. Me in a room filled with potential gang members and a male ex-con regaling the students with stories of prison life and throat punching.

Every day was a fight, it was a struggle to get content through, get the kids not to retaliate and try to work with an administration who seemed to lose sight of what their teachers needed. That year I had a student who was sexually assaulted, students who were in and out of juvenile detention, and those who couldn't wait to get arrested to hopefully earn their badge of honor.

I realized in that moment that I was no longer a teacher, I hadn't been one that whole year. I was now a prison warden, and my life was like an episode of "Orange is the New Black."

For some reason being 30 was a big deal for me. I did the typical

30 year old assessing of what I had accomplished in my life and where I saw myself in the next 30 years. I realized I hadn't slept in about a year, I had been steadily gaining weight, I was irritable, and would go to bed every night and wake up every morning with chest pains.

I was done, something had to change, but what?

I essentially spent every night searching through other job opportunities, thinking I might leave teaching all together and pursue another career path. I applied to what felt like hundreds of positions, tweaked my resume, got advice from professionals outside of my career. Nothing hit, I got one interview out of all of it. A job that I wasn't terribly excited about.

In the interview the man asked me why I wouldn't just go into a different avenue of music and education, why I wanted to leave entirely? Honestly, I was so frustrated by my current situation that education was the last thing I wanted to do. After being offered this job, I thought about what he said, and realized that maybe he was on to something.

The truth was I didn't always hate teaching....I mean, honestly, I never really enjoyed working in the schools. There was always a difficult parent, frustrating administrators, and a combination of kids who wanted to be in your class mixed with those who were just dropped in your class.

I loved making a difference, I loved working with kids, and I loved working with those who had a passion for music and theatre. What if I could just teach those kids, get rid of the difficult parents and administrators, and do the job I always wanted to do? Get rid of the red tape and garbage that comes with the job and just teach.

So needless to say I turned down the job I was offered from my one interview and decided I would take a leap of faith.

I talked to my husband about my future plans and he was completely on board. I had been following trends in virtual education, and had wanted to jump in, but was always too scared. Jason told me this was the time to do it. "You hate your job, you're miserable, and you want to make a change. This is your opportunity."

Armed with my newfound passion and direction, I sent in my letter of resignation. The minute I hit send, I felt a huge weight had been lifted. I think it was the first time I was able to breathe in almost a year. I finished out that school year with just a couple months left, and walked out of that building for the last time in May.

The next part of my journey would be the beginning of my passion becoming a reality. I was going to build a business from the ground up, finally get back to teaching, work with students in a global capacity, and be happy again.

I figured in about two years when my business was stable we would start a family, something we had been talking about. I would be able to stay home with my kids and run my own business. I was going to be able to have my cake and eat it too!

HAVE A PLAN

I've always been told the three big stressors in life are getting married, moving, and finding a new big job. This makes sense as these are huge life changes, that ultimately change the trajectory of your life.

When I was 25 I did all three of these things at once. I was getting married, at this point I will have moved twice - to a different house and then a different state, and quit my job to find a new one in my new hometown. Most of this I had actually found pretty exciting, but it was definitely some big changes in my life.

Many people I meet don't like change, it's scary and unsettling. What happens if you jump from the frying pan into the fire? What happens if you fail? What happens if you find yourself unhappy or in a situation or place you don't like? What happens if things don't turn out the way you envision them?

Well, then you make another change. It's that simple.

I understand that making big jumps isn't as easy as it sounds. It certainly wasn't for me at 30 when I was faced with some major life decisions, what do I do now?

I am a person who has always identified herself through her career. When my career was falling apart other parts of my life quickly followed and I didn't know who I was or what I was going to do next. It's a scary, unsettling feeling to have the sensation that you don't have control.

That's when it's important to start making a plan. Start identifying what makes you so unhappy and what you need to fix.

I'm not normally a journaling kind of person. I start and then usually quit because I lose interest. I had decided that every night I would write down one positive thing that happened in my day, one thing I felt needed to change, my weight, and daily exercise.

Well what I started learning was as time went on my positive section was almost non-existent. Most days I had nothing but negative commentary to write. I also noticed my weight started steadily increasing.

One day, I was in a meeting where our principal asked us to share a positive accomplishment from the year, in front of the whole faculty. I had a reputation of having a myriad of positive accomplishments, good data, and awesome news to report. Like I said earlier, I felt like all I did that year was keep the peace and keep myself and everyone else from drowning.

As he looked around with no hands going up, I made it a point to avoid eye contact. I really didn't want to be called on, I had no idea what I was going to say. As I wracked my brain for one positive thing, he called my name and asked if I had anything to share. I had to politely say, "I'm sorry I don't have anything to add today."

He looked completely shocked, and I felt completely defeated. This was the first time in my eight years as a teacher that I felt I hadn't made any difference.

As I reflected back on my journals and this experience it became clear what needed to be changed. I needed to change my job, my environment, and learn what made me happy again.

I understand most people can't just up and quit their job and start a new life. People have bills to pay and mouths to feed. Responsibilities slowly start to take over, and some people lose sight of who they are and what made them excited in the first place.

Bound and determined to not lose anymore of who I was I started coming up with a plan. At this point in my life I had been married for five years. My husband and I were both working, we had no kids, a dog, a love for travel, and endless house projects.

We worked very hard in our first five years of marriage to pay off debt. We managed to pay off our mortgage, credit card debt, and lower our expenses. Our big goal that year was to start building a sturdy nest egg and putting any extra money towards retirement. We wanted to start building a family and wanted to have a sturdy financial foundation.

When I started talking about making a career change this was incredibly helpful to know that we didn't have debt hanging over our heads. We acknowledged that we would have to put any big savings plan to the side and put all of our money towards living expenses and floating us until my new venture would take off.

Just a heads up people say that a business can take three to five years to bring in money. This also depends on what type of business you're going into, your expenses, your audience, and how quickly you grow. I had it in my head that I would be replacing my paycheck that Fall so it wouldn't be a big deal. Oh I'm a funny lady!
My husband was a little more realistic about the whole process. He was incredibly supportive. It's so important to have a strong support system if you are choosing to make a life-altering decision. If you are married it's super important to talk about any and all changes before you make them. Your life decisions will affect your spouse and family.

When I had decided to leave my position, I had told one of my co-workers, as we were in the same department. I thought it would be a nice courtesy, as my leaving would affect him as well. The next day he came to work telling me that he was planning on resigning as well. I asked him if he had a job lined up, and what his wife thought about the whole process.

There was no job lined up, his wife was totally against it, and they had four children with him being the sole bread-winner. I remember talking to him in great detail not to resign, wait until you find something, and definitely don't go against your wife's wishes. Well, he did it anyway.

I believe a couple weeks before the new school year had begun he was hired at another school. A mere year later, I was receiving a request for a reference from new jobs he was applying for. The problem was he didn't have a plan, just jumped and had to take the first job that came his way to support his family.

This is what you absolutely want to avoid. Don't leave something until you have a plan in place, support, and know what your next step is. You may not be able to jump out right away. Maybe you can start small, start a side hustle, continue to interview and apply to new jobs. Make sure to go after what you want and not just leave something out of panic.

Emotions are a funny thing, and when we do something out of sheer emotion we normally look back later with regret. It's important to acknowledge your emotions and then figure out what your next move is going to be.

After a lot of soul searching I decided to open my own business. It was definitely going to be a risky move. I had considered the risks, I had talked to my husband and family, and I had analyzed our finances. For us, this was the best decision.

The only thing was I had never started a business. Being an entrepreneur you quickly learn there is no guidebook. Instead, a lot of on the job training and individual research.

BUILDING A
BUSINESS PLAN

I never built a business, never even considered going into business. When I was in high school getting ready to pick my college major I remember having business suggested to me. I thought, "no way!"

My only knowledge of business was the concept of sitting in an office, in an isolated cubicle, working on the computer, watching the clock tick away. I thought that business was math and numbers, and I absolutely hated math and numbers! Essentially, I thought business was where creativity went to die.

I wanted to do something creative and fulfilling, where I could be amongst people and continue to grow my passion for life.

Fast forward from my sixteen year old self to my 30 year old self, and imagine the surprise from my family and friends when I said I was going to open my own business.

My perception of the world and work in general had completely shifted. As cliché as this sounds, shows like "Sharktank" gave me inspiration. I saw people who were passionate about a product they got to create. I saw people of all ages and backgrounds in front of these "Sharks" talking about how they had a vision and built something from the ground up.

What I learned was business was not soul-crushing work where creativity went to die, it was quite the opposite. Creativity was flourishing, people were truly passionate.

I heard stories of individuals leaving jobs they hated to pursue a passion they loved. They had never worked so hard in their lives, but they had also never been so happy. This was their vision and they could finally see it growing and coming to life.

I started reading many blogs, talking to people who had taken the leap to become entrepreneurs. I talked to people in the music industry, as well as industries who were completely opposite of what I was going into. I learned a great deal from each of them.

I learned their backstories, what they had to do to get to where they were. They were all gracious enough to share some words of wisdom and advice with me.

Armed with this newfound knowledge I was pretty sure I was ready to start this grand new business-venture. However, I would need to slow down and start from the planning stages.

I talked to my brother and sister who both got their degrees in business and they started asking to see my business plan. I realized I didn't have a plan, how would I write one?

Lucky for me, my sister had completed a very thorough business plan for one of her class finals. She lent it to me to peruse and get some ideas from. Even though we weren't in the same arena, Maddie in fashion, me in music, I was able to pull a great deal of information and gain an understanding of what a business plan really was.

There was so much I hadn't even thought of. I was so proud of all of the knowledge I had attained and all of the people I talked to, but never actually sat down to organize all of this information.

That summer was quite an eye opening experience for me. Conquering my first task of writing my plan took me a great deal of time and soul searching. I realized I had to start to think of things like my target market, my exact product and services, how much I was going to charge, what hosting and telecommunication platforms I would use, and how to actually teach online.

Every day I spent hours researching, writing, and planning. My plan was arduous, long, and thorough. Looking back on it now, I could have easily shortened it, but when you don't have the experience, you agonize over every last detail.

I'm a perfectionist, when I don't know something I research and struggle until I can understand or master said concept. While looking back on this plan and thinking, "April this may have been a slight overkill" it was exactly what I needed at the time.

I needed focus, I needed organization, and I needed structure. If I was truly going to leave a full time stable job to start a business I better do it right.

My plan helped me to see who I was looking for, what I wanted to become, and how I saw myself serving my future clients. I developed policies and procedures, found my website platform, planned for the future, and developed the strategies I would use to run my business.

This gave me so much excitement and purpose. I realized that I was in the driver's seat. Everything I loved about teaching, music, and theatre were going to be front and center. I would be able to leave everything I hated about my previous job behind me.

This would take quite a while, to transition between teacher and business owner. I had to learn to let go of the rules the school systems put in place and all of the minutia of being an educator. These rules no longer applied to me. I was creating my own set of rules. This is both invigorating and terrifying at the same time.

I don't necessarily like being told what to do, I love being independent. I don't need someone else to hold me accountable, I put enough pressure and standards on myself. The moment I realized that I was completely alone, and about to embark on a solo mission while creating my own set of rules and guidelines was a little unnerving.

However, the more time and experience you get the more comfortable you get with being independent, and other's rules don't matter to you anymore. Now you've tasted success and now you can say you're on your way. This takes time, we'll come back to this later in the book.

My original business plan was 36 pages long. I had found a free template online. I liked that it was super thorough. However, much of what was in the plan was not necessary for the kind of business I was about to create. I also over planned.

One of my biggest downfalls was thinking that I could do it all, and that I would be a solution for everyone. The truth is, you are not a solution for everyone because not everyone wants your product. It's a little hard to hear, but you're not everyone's cup of tea. Not because you're bad, or your product isn't quality, but it may not pertain to their life or their interests.

Since my first day of writing my plan, I learned how to be concise, a quality I usually don't possess. If you haven't learned already, I can be an incredibly wordy person. Writing this book has been a struggle to stay exactly on topic and not include too much minutia. I digress.

As I mentioned earlier I was trying to break into a new world, but only had experience in one arena. This is a problem for anyone working in a particular field for an extended period of time. Whether it's education or not, you are trained to think and work a certain way.

When I was first conceiving my business I was going to offer private lessons, group classes, curriculum for teachers, curriculum for independent learners, prerecorded video classes, webinars, and public speaking engagements. I was bound and determined to write and create all of my own content to use in each and every one of my courses and products.

The problem with this is that there's only one of me, I don't have the time or the resources to be everything to everyone. Honestly, it was a bit confusing for customers. Who was I, what was I offering?

My whole, "I will appeal to everyone everywhere," was a bit overwhelming. I would learn that down the pipeline. Much of what I learned was a lot of trial and error.

I learned a great deal in my first year. I had to learn what my customers really wanted, identify my target audience, get to know them, and learn how to connect to them. I learned what I really liked and what I simply didn't enjoy doing.

My husband gave me my biggest piece of advice when starting out which was that "time is your most valuable asset. Enjoy the time you have now, learn and grow. One day you're going to be super busy and wish you had this time back. Don't rush it." I still think back to this fairly often, because he was absolutely right. Time is my most valuable asset, now-a-days I am very picky with how and who I spend my time.

As time went on and I grew to focus, those 36 pages started to change a great deal. I started to see my new career in a new light and started to watch it evolve. With each new customer and new experience I grew a little more.

I once heard Dave Ramsey say, "you don't know what you don't know." Some pretty powerful stuff there. It's okay not to know everything. You will grow and learn as you go, if you allow yourself the time and be open to new ideas.

One of the classes I currently teach is called "How To Be An Entrepreneur." I have my students create and build a fictional business from the ground up. One of their first tasks to do is to create a business plan. The plan I wrote for them is two pages long. That's right people, two pages! The plan itself is included in the next two pages and gives an outline with definitions as well as a blank document for you to fill out. Give it a try....remember your plan may change and evolve, that's okay! You've got to start some-where. When you are armed with a plan you will find much more success in your endeavors.

Business Plan Outline - Key Essentials

Elevator Pitch: In two sentences describe your business, what you do, and what makes you unique.

Market Need - Problem You Are Solving: What is the problem that your business aims to solve? Why does your business need to exist?

Your Solution: What is the solution to the problem you just men-tioned about? What product or services will you provide and why is better than what is already out there?

Target Market / Audience: Who is your ideal customer...
Age
Gender
Buying Habits
Location
Needs
Financial Situation

Competition: List three businesses who are offering similar prod-ucts or services. List how you are different and / better than them.

Sales Channels: How will you sell your products....Do you have an online store, a physical store, both, vendors?

Marketing: How will you market your products and get the word out there. Will you buy advertising space - if so where, will you use social media, word of mouth, hand out fliers, mail advertisements, subscriptions. Will you have to have a mix according to your target market?

Team: Who will you need on your team? Are you a solopreneur? Do you need to hire people, if so, what roles are you looking for and how many do you need of each?

Milestones: Make a list of major tasks you need to complete to get your business up and running. Will you complete tasks on your own or delegate?

Budget and Sales Goals: How much is it going to cost to start up and run your business? How many sales do you need to be successful?

Business Plan Outline - Key Essentials

Elevator Pitch:

Market Need - Problem You Are Solving:

Your Solution:

Target Market / Audience: Who is your ideal customer...

Age
Gender
Buying Habits
Location
Needs
Financial Situation

Competition:

1.

2.

3.

Why you:

Sales Channels:

<u>Marketing:</u>

<u>Team:</u>

<u>Milestones:</u>

LEARNING TO EMBRACE WHAT YOU DON'T KNOW AND GROW

The desire to be profound and start something that no one had ever seen or experienced before is what every entrepreneur wants to accomplish. I can't tell you the number of times I have sat there and thought is this stuff good? Do people need to hear this? Do I sound knowledgable and experienced?

I still ask myself these questions to this day. This book has made me question that many times. I have rewritten many a paragraph in this book wondering if it's really what someone needed to hear. Will it make a difference?

The answer is yes! It does make a difference. Everyone enters stages in their lives at different times with different levels of experience and knowledge. There's so much fear out there to admit that we don't have all of the answers. We don't know everything. We don't have experience in every facet of every industry. That's perfectly okay. Experience and knowledge come, as long as you're open to it.

The more I talk to people and tell them about my journey, the more I realize I didn't know much of what I was doing or getting myself into. Honestly, the only thing I really knew was my subject-matter and general profession I was going to pull from.

The funniest thing I think about was the fact that I was going to open a virtual school for the performing arts with absolutely zero virtual teaching or even virtual communication experience. At that point I hadn't used any telecommunication platforms to casually talk to people, but now I was going to base my entire business on this concept.

I had zero coding experience and no knowledge of how to even build a website. This would also be incredibly important as my business was virtual and had no brick and mortar location.

Essentially, I was walking into a situation with zero practical experience. Man, oh man, did I learn. I have amazing people in my life who would help me and set up practice meetings so I could play with the technology and see how things worked and learn what I liked and didn't like.

After some research I found that I didn't have to know how to code. So many different hosting sites offered drag and drop designing. I was able to design a website myself that would fit the needs of my business and my future clients.

Solutions to my problems started to come once I started asking for help and taking the initiative to learn what I didn't know. The truth of the matter is, you don't have to have all of the answers and experience right away. You do, however, have to know how to find them and be willing to continue to grow.

I was pretty sure that if I had admitted failure to not knowing something or having experience in every facet of my new profession I wouldn't be taken seriously or that people would have doubts about my abilities as a professional. I didn't want to come off as ignorant or inexperienced.

I started learning and exploring different ventures that interested me. I learned I was so much more than just a teacher. Not that there's anything wrong with choosing to focus on one item or profession. I realized I loved to write, to public speak, to motivate others. I started offering different class options that encompassed some of my newfound passions.

As I started expanding my offerings, I expanded my expertise. I learned as much as I taught. I was able to reach a new audience and group of people, as well as make sure that I wasn't just "type casting" myself. Obviously, I didn't want to go totally out in left field, but I felt like I was getting a taste of different things I didn't even know existed.

I also started meeting some amazing people from all over the world. You would be shocked by the different people out there who are doing their own thing. I now have contacts in different states and countries. Some of whom I speak to, run ideas by, collaborate with, and who simply help to inspire me.

Many of them have stories similar to mine. They are constantly learning and expanding what makes them tick. The exciting commonality that all of us have is this idea that we can wear multiple hats and be multiple things.

Many times when you work in an industry you define yourself by your role, what you do. That role is usually pretty uni-singular. If you allow yourself to explore other parts of your life and personality, you may find that this opens you up to other ventures. These ventures may be a side-hustle, a new hobby, or a new career. It's more important to identify yourself by what you enjoy and what you do, rather than a single task or role you perform.

Many of my friends have started growing their families. I've watched several of them choose to open up their own businesses. They are staying home with their kids but have also created a passion project. Some of these are simply for self-gratification, others are to bring a little extra cash into the household, and some are full-fledged money making businesses.
When people chose to have a family, it's super important that both parents continue to advance themselves and their passions.

How many times do you hear people who have lost sight of who they are as individuals and once the kids leave they are lost? They don't know how to be themselves anymore or even be a couple. It's not selfish to find time to self-actualize and be a parent. Remember, you can have your cake and eat it too!

Some people have trouble identifying what they're good at. Maybe they have so many things they enjoy, passions they pursue or talents they posses. The trick is to identify what you can do for long periods of time, and get paid for.

Some things you do are hobbies, and you would grow to hate if it turned into your job. That's something to consider right off of the bat. If something is just for fun and you don't want to make it your life's work, then keep it just for fun.

That being said, you should love your new venture. My dad always told me he loved what he did so much that he's never worked a day in his life. He loved going to work, and he loved what he did, it never felt like a job or something he had to do. The minute it does, something has to change.

You should love what you do so much so that it doesn't feel like you're working. You will be putting a lot of time and energy into this facet of your life. If you don't think you'll enjoy doing something for long periods of time, then keep it as a hobby. You should feel like you can't live without doing this, the minute those feet hit the floor you're excited about the possibilities that await you.

FINDING YOURSELF AGAIN

I've always been a super strong, independent and driven person. I have a zest for life, have always been super positive, and am always striving for what's next.

I grew up in a very loving family, two parents who were clearly in love with each other who did everything they could to make sure my brother, sister, and I had a great life filled with opportunity.

My parents always taught us that life was an adventure. Sometimes even the mundane everyday tasks could be fun. There is joy in everything you do.

They raised us to believe that we could be anything and do anything as long as we set our minds to it, and worked hard for what we wanted. I credit a lot of who I am and what I have accomplished to them.

We had a very strong work ethic instilled in us from a young age. We had responsibilities, chores, and when we turned 16 years old were expected to get a job. We had to keep good grades, get involved in activities and still set aside time to spend with family.

When it was time to go to college, the deal for all three of us kids was our parents would pay for half of our college and it was our responsibility to pay for the rest. They didn't care if it was through cash or scholarships. It turned out all three of use received half-ride scholarships through our chosen colleges and universities.

The second stipulation was that we kept our scholarships, completed degrees in four years, and didn't fail any classes. The failing of a class was on us to repeat and pay for. Anything after four years was completely on us, and any scholarship money lost was ours to reimburse. The goal was work hard, play hard. If you couldn't figure out how to balance the two, you'd learn.

Let me tell you, it worked. We all kept our end of the bargain, graduated in four years, and moved on to successful careers.

My parents were a big fan of imparting some life lessons, many times in the form of phrases that would be on constant repeat and become a life mantra. I mean as kids we would roll our eyes, or recite it back to them, like "yeah, yeah, yeah we've heard this a hundred times." I can honestly say I don't think I fully understood the messages until much later in my life.

These life lessons would prove imperative in my adult years. Especially during my desire to go out on my own.

Honestly, it should be noted that my mom is probably reading this and completely mortified that some of these made it into this book. However, they were useful and stuck with me. At least you know I was listening Mom. Growing up, if we whined and naturally accused our parents of having no sympathy the famous quote would be "you want sympathy look in the dictionary between shit and syphilis, that's where you'll find sympathy."

I've never actually been able to quote this exactly as she does. There might be a slight discrepancy, but you get the picture. Whining was an absolute no go in our house. If you whined, it was almost guarantee that you weren't going to get what you wanted.

This was something I found myself doing in my teaching. I didn't say this phrase to students, but I did find myself squelching whining right away. "We don't do that here." My students learned very quickly, if you wanted something, vocalize what it is you want and be proactive. Whining is a waste of time and energy.

This famous phrase in combination with a principle that I hold dear to this day. When bad things happen you get 24 hours to yell, scream, feel sorry for yourself, cry, eat, whatever you need to do. Once those 24 hours are up, it's action time. It's time to take the emotion and whatever the situation you're facing and fix it. You're not going to sit there and pout and let the negativity consume you, instead you're going to pick yourself up and show the world what you've got. You can only be knocked down if you allow it.

This is important, repeat that to yourself..... "You can only be knocked down if you allow it."

At 30 years old the hard facts were I was absolutely getting knocked down and lost site of the positives. I had totally let more than 24 hours roll by. I wasn't stuck, I just couldn't see the forest from the trees. I was so consumed with the day to day negativity that I found myself in, that I could no longer see all the positives I had going for me and the other options I had.

When I finally acknowledged this, my world changed. I didn't have to live like this, and as hard as it was to hear, I was part of the problem. Until I was ready to change my mindset and get back the tenacity, passion, and fight that was such a part of who I was, nothing would change. The moment I decided my life would change, it did.

Another life lesson growing up that always stayed with me was this idea of choices. My dad would always tell us, "life is about choices. The more positive choices we make, the more opportunities are available to us. The more negative choices we make, opportunities start to dwindle." In addition, a simple word, the most important "F" word in the English language....."Focus." Keep your eye on the prize and focus on what you want.

This was something I would watch play out as a day-to-day truth.

I would see friends, acquaintances, and family members who made a myriad of life choices, some good, some not so good. I started paying attention to how their lives turned out. It became abundantly clear who I wanted to emulate and those who became cautionary tales.

I started recognizing other things I didn't care for. I was done with negative people and situations. There was no reason to keep these people in my life. People who were constantly complaining, lived for drama, or only saw the negative in life were booted out. Negativity drags you down, and negative people don't bring anything to the table. When you make the cut, new groups of people are allowed to enter your life.

I started to dream again, plan for my future and get fired up for what was to come.

Over these last three years of being independent I have had more opportunities than I could have dreamed of. I have met some of the most amazing people this world has to offer. I get to pair my love of travel, the arts, performance, teaching, business, writing, inspiring, and speaking together. I'm still constantly learning and evolving and am more excited than ever.

Not only did I get a zest for life back, but I got to rediscover myself. I finally found that person I loved and got to share that with other people.
In addition to all of the exciting things going on professionally, this year 2018 / 2019 we found out we were expecting our first child. Maizy Ann Vargo is due on June 7, 2019. Once this book comes out she'll definitely be here and living her best life.

It was another venture my husband and I were looking forward to pursuing. Growing our family from just he and I, adding a dog a couple years into our marriage, and now 8 years into our marriage adding a little girl.

BUILDING A LIFESTYLE

Once you find yourself settled, happy, and executing your plan, you also want to make sure to keep in mind the lifestyle you want to build. Making a big change, creating a new venture, and building your life is fabulous. However, you want to make sure you're building towards the life you want to live, otherwise you'll find yourself in another rut.

I'm sure you have the ideal picture of a life you're hoping to live. Maybe it's sitting on the porch drinking coffee as the sun comes up, working in your adorable new outfits while sitting on the couch under your favorite blanket, traveling the world, or simply getting to spend time with your family. Whatever your vision is, make sure you build towards that dream.

I remember when I first started I read countless blogs of what a successful entrepreneur does with their day. I studied different schedules and wanted to follow advice of how others succeeded.

The overwhelming majority of people seemed to say how much they worked. Get up early and work until sundown. Make sure you're available at all times via phone, email, and social media. Take everyone who's interested in your product, a sale is a sale.

I found all of this to be untrue. My ideal life was not to glued to my device, working nonstop, and building a clientele of people I may or may not like. Let's be honest, we all want to make money, we all have bills to pay, and we all want to but successful. However, there are multiple ways to accomplish this goal.

I quickly started setting up guidelines for myself. I wanted a life where I could work, build a family, travel, socialize, have times for hobbies and other projects that interested me. Here's what I came up:

- I will schedule classes Monday - Thursday, times are relatively flexible
- Friday is an open day for appointments, interviews, pet projects, paper work, advertising, accounting, and travel
- Evenings and weekends are my time
- I have a 24 hour communication policy, I will return your email within 24 hours
- I don't give out my cell phone number to the masses, email only
- I do not schedule make up lessons, you cancel or no show, you miss the lesson and an alternate means of make up is available
  - The missing student sends a recording of them completing that week's assignment and I will send feedback on what to work on for the next lesson
- Payment needs to be received before a lesson or class can be scheduled
- Students need to come to class with enthusiasm, passion, and a willingness to learn and work hard

These guidelines became the building blocks of my business and life-style. Guess what, parents and students respected and abided by them. By me being fair and upfront, they always knew what was going on and what to expect. They get a quality product and my undivided attention, however, I also get to have a life outside work.

All of this is listed on my website as well. There is no guess work, no one feels like they're being screwed, and people know what they are entering into when they begin.

These guidelines came into play through years of working with various types of people, and learning how some people treat professionals. Sometimes people feel that if they pay for a product or service they get to dictate the rest of your life or tell you how to run your business. Nope, not here. If you let people run your life or business, they will absolutely do so.

In laying it out there right from the beginning I have also been able to develop a rapport with my students and their families. I started learning I was getting serious people coming through my door. I had students from beginners to working professionals. I noticed I was getting repeat customers and was building a successful clientele. My students can be found in all 50 US States, Canada, New Zealand, Australia, South Korea, South America, and Europe.

I started developing a relationship with students and their families. I was getting emails and texts from students telling me how their days went, something positive that happened in their lives, that they just go the role they were hoping for, and how they had achieved their goals. I started to learn that my job became so much more than just a job, I was building a community. In building a community I was also able to build a life for myself.

I am able to spend time with my family, travel, take on projects that interest me, pursue hobbies and still build a business I love. My life is full, happy, and successful. In order to get there, boundaries needed to be set. Don't be afraid to ask for what you want, and set standards from day one. It's a lot easier to start out with standards versus going back and trying to change things after you have a regular clientele.

THE JOURNEY

The journey to making a change and going out on your own is not easy, but it's worth it. Even though I started off this book in earlier chapters talking about planning, it is important to know that not everything goes according to plan. It's so important to remain flexible and keep yourself open to change and new opportunities.

You'll learn that you are constantly growing. The journey itself is filled with many ups and downs. I remember when I first started I thought that I would build this awesome business in a summer, release it, and people would flock to me. I would have made up my paycheck in no time at all and be living my best life.

Well that's not exactly how it went. I released my initial website and no one came. I got a lot of compliments and lot of, "you go girl," but not one sale. I had several hurdles to overcome:

- Learning how to properly price and sell my products
- Focus on my offerings
- Educate people on what virtual education and lessons were
- Getting in front of the right people

In my first year, I brought in $1000.00. Mind you, I was pretty sure I was a millionaire because I had never worked so hard for $1000.00 in my life. Now, after expenses I took a loss that year.

I remember feeling super guilty. What had I just put our family through, what if I failed, and what if I put my husband and I in a bad situation? The truth of the matter was a business takes time to build. Jason was well aware of this and wasn't shocked in the least. I, on the other hand, had just been given a dose of reality.

Some days were lonely, as you go from working with people to being independent and at home alone. The vision I was pursuing was very unique so it was difficult to get any direct feedback or advice from people.

When you start out, this new idea and concept is very much like the beginning of a life. It's something that you plan for, cultivate, and tailor the rest of your life to function around. As you launch the business you have an idea of what you would like it to be like, how you envision its future. Many times it doesn't go according to the plan, it's usually better than you imagined.

The beginning of my business was definitely not as focused as I thought. When I look back I was basically mimicking the roles and functions I had done while being employed and bringing that to the masses. The problem was, it was overwhelming, no one really understood what it was I did.

I thought, "oh maybe I just need to do more explaining about what it is I do. I mean people love options, right?" The reality is, people don't like options. It sounds weird, but think about the classic questions of "where do you want to eat tonight?" Many times one or both people don't really have an opinion, tell the other whatever you want is fine, shoot down every option you mention because they just don't have a taste for that, or vacillate so much that you just eating what's around the house.

If you would have taken the same scenario and said do you want pizza or chicken, more often than not someone would have an opinion. It's not an open-ended question, there's two clear options, and it gives someone an idea off of the bat. This is the same when you decide to offer too much or a great deal of customization, people get overwhelmed and walk away.

I found this out the hard way. It was difficult to get in front of the right people. I went through all types of situations, I tried giving free trial lessons, went to vendor conferences, and did a great deal of cold calling. The problems I ran into across the board were people who weren't serious about what I had to offer. They'd be all about pursuing opportunities if they were free, but paid for services were a no go.

I realized that I had to get in the mindset of the people I wanted to work with. I knew these people, I was one of these people. Instead of throwing massive amounts of junk against a wall, I started to get selective. I started asking myself who I was and what was it I truly enjoyed doing? What were my strengths? How could I use my strengths to build a business with a clientele I loved?

First step, I stopped giving away products and services for free. If you weren't interested enough to pay for them, you weren't interested enough in what I had to offer. This helped me to be selective and go after a clientele I really wanted to work with.

What I realized was I started getting interested customers. I started building relationships with other organizations who had heard about me and wanted to bring my programs on board. I brought on students who have stayed with me for the long haul, and are passionate about what they wanted. This helped to develop long-lasting, meaningful relationships. This also helped me to see that being picky was actually bringing my business to life.

I was definitely criticized by people saying that you have started a new business, you don't have the luxury to be picky, you have to take whoever comes through that door. I felt completely opposite. I didn't have the luxury to be miserable again. This was my business, my dream, and I wasn't going to let it turn into something I despised.

Good people don't want subpar service, they don't want to work with non-committal individuals. They want quality, and they want to work with quality people. When you start advertising, "I only work with quality, I don't take everyone"....ding, ding, ding you speak to these individuals.

I actually just created a relationship with a realtor, public speaker, and business owner. The biggest "selling point" she had was I don't beg for clients. I work with people who are interested in working with me, and I only accept quality people. Right then and there, I looked at my husband and said we will be working with her.

You don't need to beg for people to come to you, have a good product, be a good person, and deliver stellar services, people will come.

This was one of the big ways my business started to develop. As I started growing my clientele I started to learn what it was they wanted and needed. I started to develop relationships and programs around the progress they were making.

Again, people started hearing about what I was doing. I started getting connected with other names of professionals who were independent, and I started getting invited to participate in different opportunities. I have spoken at an international music education conference, directed many live theatre productions, been invited on many radio shows, podcasts, and joined different teams for various projects.

My business started to reflect the work I was doing. I would publicize and talk about my new ventures and relationships, and the business would continue to grow.

I learned that I really loved different subject-matters such as public speaking, entrepreneurship, and confidence building classes on top of my music and theatre offerings. I started building and teaching classes with those subject-matters as well. The more interests I had, the more I would throw myself deeper into my work.

My husband would often ask me, do you have the experience to teach some of these subjects? I quoted a teacher I had who gave me some great advice, "if you know more than the people you're teaching, then you can teach." I'm not claiming to be an expert in all of these fields, but I certainly had more experience than those I was teaching.

The more I taught and researched and took myself out of my comfort zone, the more I learned and explored, and improved my skills. I was getting actual experience on the job. Then I was getting to share my newfound experience and knowledge right away.

My website was constantly changing and evolving with the new offerings I was creating. The business and I were changing together. If you watched one you could see the evolution of the other.

I was just talking to someone the other day, saying I'm still evolving, I haven't quite finished this project. Play.Sing.Act is close to what I want it to be, but I'm not done tweaking. I have so many different ideas, some of which may fall under this business, and maybe in the future I expand into other endeavors as well. That's the exciting part, is we, as people, are never done exploring and evolving. If you're stagnant, you're dead. Keep moving and creating.

Each year, I started watching my paycheck increase, I was actually in the black and was able to start contributing to our household. This was huge for me. I wanted to be able to feel independent and that I was helping our household as well.

It was super exciting when a year ago my husband went out independently to open his own business as well. I started to realize I now got to be his cheerleader and was able to help our family as he navigated the new world of independence.

I often think of what would have happened if I didn't make the jump. Our lives would be so different now. The future is super exciting with nothing but potential and opportunities ahead.

APRIL'S WORDS OF WISDOM

This book was not intended to be a long novel that would take you weeks upon weeks to read. Let's be honest, life happens, you'll start reading, put it down, and most likely never come back to it. I am guilty of doing this many a times.

This book is instead, meant to be concise, easy, and thought-provoking. I want it to spark a fire for someone who is looking for more. I am hoping to share some of my knowledge and experience and help you get the ball rolling today. It's meant to be a bit of a taste of what's out there, and help you to have your cake and eat it too.

That mantra was something that always stuck with me. So many people always say, "you can't have your cake and eat it too." I always asked why not? The idea is you can have it all if you want to work for it and have the drive and passion to succeed.

In closing up the book I definitely wanted to share some words of wisdom that I have learned. These are principles I live by on a daily basis. I hope these help you as you navigate your journey:

1. Always be true to yourself.

Everyone has dreams and ambitions, and they matter. Don't let them fall to the wayside because life happens. Instead, find a way to work them into your life. Maybe you can't quit your job tomorrow and start a new venture. Maybe it's going to take some time. However, you can start making changes today, start a side hustle, start a hobby, join that gym, make friends, date that cutie, the list goes on and on..... At the end of the day, do what makes you happy.

2. Be open to new adventures.
Be careful to put too many guidelines and rules on yourself. So many people limit themselves or try to put themselves into a box. I mean, you have to be focused and have a plan. Sometimes events can happen that will make you deviate from that plan, be flexible. Be willing to get outside of your comfort zone and try new things. Say yes more than you say no. You'll find that you grow and prosper in ways you would never have imagined.

3. Set goals.
I'm a huge goal setter, it's so important to have something to constantly work towards. You should be setting short and long term goals. Set up ways to track your goals and hold yourself accountable. Give yourself a realistic amount of time to achieve said goals so you can be successful. When you achieve and realize success, reflect back on your process. Ask yourself what went well, and what were some things you could improve upon? Self-reflection and critiquing is incredibly important for continued growth.

4. Develop a lifestyle.
Your work should not eat up your entire life. If you're working 24 hours a day, 7 days a week you will burn yourself out and let other facets of your life fall. Instead, build your job around the lifestyle you want to lead. Set standards and parameters. Don't be afraid to tell people what you want and how you want to live. People will respect your parameters and will work with you. You will be happy and fulfilled.

5. Always look forward.

Life is an adventure. It's constantly moving, and moving rather quickly. Don't focus on the past, learn from it, let it motivate you, and move forward. Do things that challenge you and push you to be a better person. Dream big, and tell people of your plans. People will rally behind you and genuinely celebrate when you succeed.

6. Always be kind.

Be kind to everyone you meet. You never know the struggles people are going through. You don't have to be a pushover or be taken advantage of, but try and approach every situation with a clear head. Think before you speak. Be fair and consistent. At the end of the day people will remember how you made them feel, not necessarily what you taught them.

Remember you can have your cake and eat it too!

www.ingramcontent.com/pod-product-compliance
Lightning Source LLC
Chambersburg PA
CBHW071445170526
45158CB00005BA/1837